D. R. Toi
223 Southlake Pl.
Newport News, VA

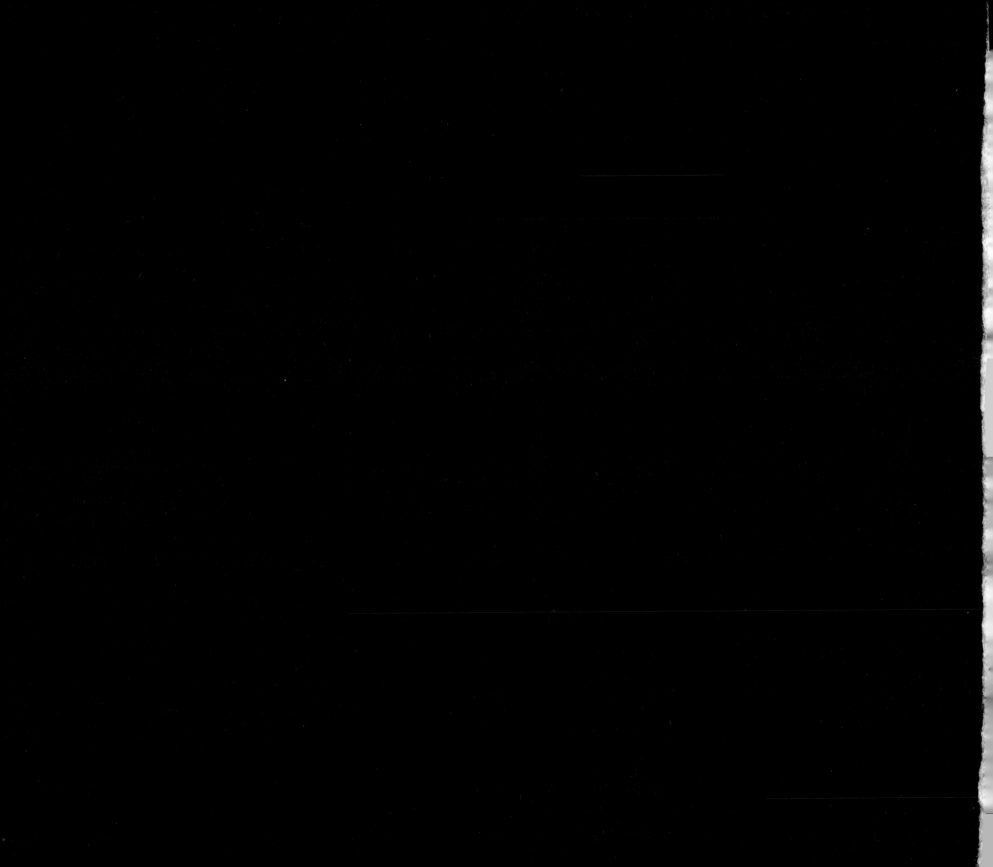

Worlds of Spirit

A SEQUENCE OF COSMIC PERSPECTIVES

Bô Yin Râ is the author of a cycle of thirty-two works, titled *Hortus Conclusus (The Enclosed Garden)*. The following other works of that cycle are available in English translation:

> *The Book on the Living God*
> *The Book on Life Beyond*
> *The Book on Human Nature*
> *The Book on Happiness*
> *The Book on Solace*
> *The Wisdom of St. John*
> *The Meaning of This Life*
> *Spirit and Form*

Also available is *Bô Yin Râ: An Introduction to His Works*.

Bô Yin Râ

Worlds of Spirit
A SEQUENCE OF COSMIC PERSPECTIVES

Translated by

B. A. Reichenbach

Berkeley, California

English translation © 2002 by B. A. Reichenbach
Eric Strauss, Publisher & Editor
All rights reserved

For permission to quote or excerpt, write to:
THE KOBER PRESS
2534 Chilton Way, Berkeley, California 94704

or email: koberpress@mindspring.com

This book is a translation from the German of the second edition (1956) of *Welten* by Bô Yin Râ (J. A. Schneiderfranken), first published in 1922. The copyright to the German original is held by Kober Verlag AG, Bern, Switzerland.

First printing limited to 500 copies
Printed in Canada
Library of Congress Control Number 2001096453
International Standard Book Number 0-915034-09-3
Type and design by Irene Imfeld, Berkeley, California

CONTENTS

Preface   1

The Ascent   7

The Return   17

Reviews of Creation   25

Epilogue   77

PREFACE

IN THE PRESENT BOOK, the visual image will accompany the written word, and thus combined, they both would help you to unlock the *soul's sublime horizon* in yourself.

A brief initial look at the included reproductions—before the written word was able to attune your soul, even as one tunes a harp—may very likely give you the impression that modern day "expressionism," which, at the time this book was written, sought to assert itself in all the arts, had also influenced the forms presented in these paintings.

Were that the case, I gladly would affirm your judgment.

In fact, however, the attempts to represent in visual form what here is now depicted, reach back into a time when the desire for such new expressiveness was still an unknown impulse in the realm of art. Besides, I must confess that I have never felt the inner need myself that has in our time compelled creative artists in all fields to search for new means of expression because the old traditions seemed no longer true and pure enough to satisfy their own creative drives.

I well can understand what may impel that inner urge and cause one to explore a new approach, but I have always found the views presented in my paintings given to me from within, and, for that matter, *with their corresponding forms*. As a result, the only inner need I ever felt was to express the very forms I had encountered in myself.

The paintings that accompany the present book originated in me in the same way as all other works that ever sought expressive form within me.

However, the realities to be depicted here were in themselves of wholly different structure, so that the impulse to present them truthfully would, of necessity, result in likewise different forms.

Being fully conscious in an inner world of *radiant, life-informing Spirit*—as much as in the realm of matter experienced through the mortal body—I know the forms depicted here as well as any we perceive by means of our earthly senses.

Yet, while material objects, illuminated by the sun on earth, will by and large remain within their static limits, in the dimensions of the Spirit's light all forms one apprehends reveal themselves, instead, in *ever active transformation*.

Here on earth all forms can be observed and represented from a single, fixed perspective; in the dimensions of the Spirit, by contrast, one beholds all forms as if one were a hollow sphere whose boundaries consisted of a thousand eyes.

Yet even here I had no need to search for special ways of presentation.

What my experience showed me would of itself become transformed into a two-dimensional image, and I sought mainly to retain what I beheld, with ever greater clarity, and freed of all extraneous elements, with the professional techniques at my command.

The titles of these paintings point to that which in this book I would awaken as the reader's own experience, through the written word.

These titles are to be considered only as descriptive hints to help the viewer find the inner state one must attain if contemplation of the images is to awaken echoes of their *harmonies and rhythms* in the viewer's soul.

The exceptional readers who, on their own, are able to experience fully conscious life in those domains of Spirit of which these paintings give account, will have no difficulty recognizing features in them which they, too, may have encountered.

Others need to bear in mind that one will not experience the dimensions of the Spirit's world depicted in these works until one long has left behind the nether realm of occult visions—that sphere of endless twilight, teeming with deceptions and demonic terrors—from which somnambulating dreamers, mediums, and ecstatics are accustomed to appeal for what they think is "proof" of the projections of their warped imagination.

Since all components represented in the spiritual perspectives of this book are, by nature, deeply rooted in the inmost core of every human soul on earth, where corresponding elements may thus be found, these paintings can awaken the *spiritual energies* that let the soul's inherent senses concentrate themselves to form that one, *all-unifying inner sense* whereby alone one can experience any ultimately true events of spiritual reality.

To awaken that all-comprehending inner sense within the reader's soul is finally the purpose that both *words* and *images* presented here are meant to serve.

The extent to which this can be realized in any given case depends exclusively on the degree of spiritual development the reader has been able to attain.

Yet much can also be accomplished simply by the right approach to seeking that attunement of one's soul.

If readers would be given what this book contains, they ought to, from the outset, leave aside all intellectual interpretations of the images presented.

One must immerse one's inmost self into their forms, to *feel* them solely from *within*; for only that can bring about the transformation of the hieroglyphs, here given visual form, into *dynamic inner energy*, which then will stir the *soul* and can be felt as such.

A vital factor here will always be the viewers' own determined will to let their feelings actively respond; for only thus may contemplation of the paintings waken echoes in the reader's soul.

Although this willingness is a prerequisite for understanding art of any kind, it here is called for to an even higher degree, in that one strives to reach one's *inner realm* through the external objects apprehended by the eye.

Once their faculty for visually perceiving inner life has actively awakened, readers doubtless will be able to experience other views as well, depending on their individual potential. Because the images provided here are but a sequence of thematically related inner sights, whose purpose, supported by the written word, is that of bringing closer to the readers' souls an inner world from which they have become far more estranged than necessary, owing to the influence of their external world.

Readers who already are acquainted with the ancient teachings of objective knowledge that I was granted to make public through my books, will have no difficulty comprehending the intention of the present work.

However, I was able to observe that even people unacquainted with my writings, especially those of some artistic sensibility, were able to experience—after not much time of learning how to "see" with feeling eyes—a *resonance* to *inner harmonies* within their souls, which found expression in awakening presentiments of timeless life.

I can and must not give the viewer "explanations" of the realm whose forms and colors wanted visual rendition in these paintings, lest I obstruct the path that every reader's soul must needs pursue in its own way.

Here I have to trust the soul's dynamic energies that every reader finds within.

All attempts to *analyze* these paintings must do harm; one thus would only bury the most vital content under veils of clouding thought.

Initiates of the hermetic arts of magic, practiced through the ages in every culture of the ancient world, had always guarded knowledge of especial sacred signs. Today, not many are aware that those particular signs were owed to *spiritual perception*, having been discovered first within the worlds of the eternally creative Spirit.

You here may see those signs at work within their timeless sphere of action.

Only if you still are able to immerse yourself into your spirit's primal nature will these signs reveal their energy within you.

Blest you are if then you comprehend their meaning—by virtue of their impact on *your soul*.

You then will have no further need to search for "explanations."

And you will bless the day that brought this book into your hands.

But I shall see your joy with gladness . . .

Bô Yin Râ

THE ASCENT

WHOEVER YOU MAY JUDGE yourself to be whose soul is seeking truth and light, take my hand and rise with me beyond the solid prison walls—to which you long since have become accustomed—wherein your body's mortal senses hold you captive, closely yoked and fettered.

All too long have you already borne your chains, so that you grew to cherish them like precious jewels, worthy to adorn a king.

Begin to comprehend that *you alone* possess the power to keep yourself in chains, and that *no other but yourself* can ever claim the keys that shall unlock your bondage.

Find the courage to forego the safety of your prison, and seize the prize of freedom—through *your own resolve!*

Let me not have unbarred the heavy door in vain that keeps you trapped within your gloomy cell.

Prepare yourself to enter on a journey to a very distant land, a realm you at this time still do not know or only fathom vaguely. Be assured, however, that I am here to guide you to your timeless *home*, the land where you were born, but which, eternities ago, you had abandoned. And now you feel its light-filled, endless spaces to be strange and frightening, because you are accustomed to seeing only dungeon walls define the limits of your vision.

You shall not have to forfeit anything that, during your captivity, you truly loved with heart and soul.

Returning, you shall find again, according to your will, whatever you have left behind; nor is there anyone who could deprive you of the least—except yourself.

But when you shall come back to this dimension, after our journey through the spheres, your gloomy cell shall be transformed into a radiant hall within a palace—and you shall then be *master of the keys*.

Everything you own today, it shall continue to be yours hereafter; only you will then have learned to put it to far better use. And what today still lies debased in squalor shall then reflect the radiant light you shall be taking with you from your timeless home, back to the twilight gloom of mortal life on earth.

I urge you: Cling no longer to this place of your captivity, and do not anxiously torment yourself with questions whether you possess the strength to follow me.

Every moment you delay will needlessly prolong your bondage.

Trust the power rooted in your inmost self! Only through your own inherent strength shall you be able freely to ascend with me.

I, however, shall be no more than your *guide*; and to that end have I been sent to find you; for you had "called" for inner light.

Have *faith*—while you can still not wholly *understand!*

Have *faith*—so that you one day may acquire *knowledge*.

Have *faith*—come forth and follow me!

✳

At last, at last, I feel your cautious hand.

Be not afraid to grasp my hand more firmly, that I may guide you safely to your goal.

Already you can sense that we are *rising* high and higher; soon you shall have risen to such heights, however, that everything you had considered "high" before shall lie infinities below us.

Already we have soared above the sphere of gloom and narrow limitations, and here your feet no longer feel the burden of your body's weight.

Far below us lies the earthly globe with all its misery and grief.

Let not your thinking dwell on what you only now have left behind; for every painful and depressing thought becomes a burden that impedes your free ascent.

Instead, your looking down should serve you as a "recoil," so that even glancing at what lies below will reinforce your energy to rise.

Regard all things you left behind as shadows of a fleeting dream that you at last have happily escaped, and which is never going to return.

Your own inherent power causes you to rise toward a completely *new* experience; but you will apprehend its essence in your being only if you can *forget* what until now had seemed to you the highest goal you could attain.

✳

Even as I speak to you I sense that you have found my words sufficient to awaken and engage your will.

Already you are borne aloft, relieved of all impediments.

Your eyes, which had but now seemed dull and lifeless, are gaining light and radiance.

Far brighter still their shine will grow as we draw closer to the Light that used to be your timeless home, which you yourself had once desired to abandon, eternities ago.

Now we are still drawn aloft through space that you believe is "empty"; for there is nothing here your senses are yet able to discern.

In fact, however, life in infinite abundance surrounds you even here; and what you deem is "empty space" appears so only to your still unpracticed vision.

Mark the truth that there exists no "empty space" in all infinities throughout creation; that all apparent "emptiness" is, in reality, replete with forms and life, and that your faculties of apprehending all this life continue to unfold the more effectively your own life can ennoble and refine itself.

*

We need to soar far higher still, through all expanses of the starry firmament.

Beyond the realms of the most distant suns must we ascend before we reach those cosmic spheres wherein your *spirit's eye* is to awaken—from a sleep you have endured for ages.

*

Already we have far exceeded even those remotest spheres which, seen from earth, appear as no more than translucent veils across the velvet sky on cloudless nights, and still our soaring flight has not yet reached its goal.

We now behold ourselves within a space of measureless expanse; and with amazement you perceive the same translucent starry veils that we have left behind and far below not only spreading also high above, but equally enclosing you on every side.

We find ourselves as if within a *sphere* of inconceivable dimensions, whose outer limits are defined by myriads of galactic systems.

But in the center of this boundless space you now behold a new and different Light: more brilliant than the brightest bolt of lightning, more radiant than the blinding sunlight shining on tropical seas.

Did I hear your first exultant shout of joy?

Indeed, there is no longer any doubt—your inner eye has opened!

✶

You grasp my hand more firmly?

It seems you are aware that everything you used to know until this day has utterly deserted you and that before all else you first must *learn to see* in this effulgent Light.

Even as the colorful auroras brilliantly illuminate the endless nights enveloping the icy poles on earth, so is the boundless sea of light, in which we now appear suspended, alive in countless rays of wondrously resplendent hues.

Your eyes are still not able to distinguish things of concrete form within the brightness of this living light.

That still needs time, and will require that we rise to yet far higher spheres.

✶

Do you already see the first cascading rays of blinding white that flash our way like vivid bolts of lighting?

Raise your eyes and look where they originate!

Do you recoil in terror?

You feel that we have long since ceased to rise through our strength alone, but that the PRIMAL SUN—whose overwhelming radiance you now espy within the very center of the boundless sphere of cosmic space—has seized us with magnetic force, to draw us irresistibly into the heart of its eternal conflagration.

✶

You now have lost your power to resist; and even while you think you are arresting your ascent, your heart all terrified and trembling, we have continued soaring ever closer to the fiery veils surrounding that primordial Sun.

✳

I understand why you should feel afraid, although it has been long since I myself had known that dread.

I, too, had once to overcome this frightening awe when, guided by another, I first experienced this domain.

Still, when I promised I would guide you back to your eternal *home*, you heard me promise final *truth*, even though your very being now is gripped by terror, fearing imminent annihilation.

✳

Again, you must not let yourself be frightened even by the deafening thunder whose resounding peals you now hear rolling towards our path.

More quickly than you would expect shall we be drawn aloft and through this "ring of terror" by the power of that primal Sun.

Remain but sure of *your own self*, and of your will's resolve to make your way back to the realm that is your timeless home.

Rid yourself of all your probing thoughts and worries, nor even feel concerned about your *life!*

Whether you are meant to live, or perish, must in your judgment be alike—if I am not to have accompanied your journey to these heights in vain.

Whatever you have been in your own judgment, whatever you have made out of your life—you must be ready willingly to sacrifice.

In this primordial sea of fire you now shall without question be *transformed*—with or against your will—but here it shall become apparent *who you truly are.*

Consumed within that cosmic fire you will be reborn as a *flaming star*, to be returned to the external world, so that your radiance may illuminate its darkness. Or—your vacillating will becomes your doom, condemning you to aeons of renewed affliction.

I never would have come to take you from your prison, nor persuaded you to undertake this flight, had you yourself not "called" me countless times before, in all those lonely nights of your captivity on earth.

Now, you have no longer any chance of turning back.

Here it shall become apparent whether you had truly earned the right to "call."

Only those who prematurely clamored for salvation may here encounter their undoing, forfeiting their conscious self-awareness in these blazing fires for eternities.

They, too, shall one day be sent forth again into eternal "space" as radiant spiritual *scintillas*. But they had not yet reached maturity to be such *flaming stars* today, and so the primal fires of the cosmic Sun, which is their final home, could not bring forth their new birth at this time, to raise them toward their highest form of being.

*

But now cast off the numbing fear that weighs upon your shoulders!

No lofty goal has ever been attained by fear.

So long as fear still rules your soul you will not find your destined place in this primordial realm—where all that *is* has its beginning—for you are not yet willing to offer your whole being as a sacrifice, and in so doing *find* your timeless self.

Do you not know the Master's words forewarning you that you shall *lose* your soul if you are anxious to *preserve* it? And that you cannot gain your timeless self unless you break the fetters that keep you chained to your own being?

∗

Although I may not at this moment give you full assurance that you truly will endure the final trial now before you, it is unlikely you would now be standing here if there were any danger of your plunging from these heights.

You hardly would have followed me when I had sought you in your cell in answer to your "calling"; for you would have expected something different, not the guidance I was sent to offer you.

Those who "called" although they knew full well they had no right, have always hid themselves within their prison's darkest vaults whenever one of us would knock upon their door. Only the most brazen recklessness has on occasion led some seekers wantonly to follow our guidance, even knowing they were not prepared.

You, on the other hand, were hesitant and followed me with caution; and so I feel that you can truly have more confidence in your own self than you might think is rightful.

Do not become your own tormentor, but trust instead your inner star.

The very *star* wherein you are to find your highest form; the star as which you shall return, transformed, having freed your timeless nature of your present self within the fires of this primal Sun.

You must no longer want to live as something other than this radiant Sun, whose fires comprehend all *Being*, all *Existence*; and through its power it shall bring you forth anew, so that within its light *your life shall be eternal.*

✶

Yet here I shall withdraw—for your perception—and you will seem alone; for I must at this point transform myself, in light and fire, as one whose sight you now would not endure.

    Within the heart of that primordial Sun I now shall take my given place. And when you find me once again, you too shall have become a star and will as such return with me into the gloomy realm of earth, in order to bring light to those who need it in their darkness.

    Unlike myself, however, you have no obligation to repeat this journey countless times; nor are you bound by any pledge to serve the duties I have shouldered. And yet, the star ablaze in you will issue from the same primordial fire that once had also granted me its radiance, long before I would encounter you in mortal form on earth.

    Enter now into your timeless home!

    Let the flames of its eternal light consume your very being—and then once more return to me, as one who is become a *child of light*!

    Within the inmost heart of this primordial Sun shall I expect your birth. And here, then, in the realms of its irradiant splendor, shall you at last behold and know your guide in his eternal nature, undisguised.

    Enter now and find your true perfection, so that a new star may be given birth; a star whose light will shine amidst the gloomy darkness and despair on earth.

✶ ✶

✶

THE RETURN

AND SO I COME TO MEET you once again, triumphant in your victory, a radiant star that now is born anew out of the splendor of eternal light.

Again we find ourselves where I had left you, in order to transform myself into this luminescent body, which now your eyes can apprehend, given that you have yourself become a being born of purest light.

You now will understand why earlier you would not have endured to see me in this transcendent form of light.

Within the same primordial fires shall we henceforth be united throughout all eternity.

And now you also comprehend why every *master* in this realm must have been *taught* by one more perfect than himself; and that the cosmic ladder formed by this eternal hierarchy cannot ever end, because the *Absolute* is in itself *Infinity*. Every "highest" level, thus, beholds one higher still above it, which will become the goal of its self-transformation, whenever it has reached its ultimate perfection.

You and I are still the lowest rungs comprising this celestial ladder.

Upon myself, as you already know, had long ago been placed the binding pledge to not abandon the eternal Spirit's *field of energy*, whose force sustains all human life on earth, until the last one of my fellow human mortals has found its way into the world of light, like you: until each one has been made part again of the hierarchic chain of stars that shine throughout eternity.

And so I now must, like yourself, return to earth and darkness. And even when my mortal garb shall one day have been laid to rest, I am not free to leave the spiritual aura that sustains mankind, as long as human souls shall live embodied on this planet.

Not so yourself; for when the chains of mortal life no longer hold you captive, you will at once begin your transformation toward the next degree, the form in which I now appear before your spirit's eye. You, however, are not obligated to remain within that form, which you experience merely as a new potential of experience. To me, by contrast, it provides the means through which my inmost self has chosen to be active.

You, having reached your highest level of perfection in that form, will then discern the next that lies above. And, once again, you shall transform yourself to reach that higher level, even as you will have changed yourself into the form that now is mine, once you have attained perfection of your present form, after having shed your mortal creature body.

This ascent toward ever higher levels of perfection does not end through all eternity. Moreover, to attain perfection at the highest level, in any of the forms that here appear above us, demands increasingly vast spans of time. Until we reach a point where our mental concept of "eternity" becomes a tiny fraction of the ages during which the higher states of being realize their ultimate perfection.

But every word of human language seeking to explain these cosmic evolutions in intelligible terms is doomed to be a helpless stammer. Not until you have attained the actual faculty that gives you insight into these events can you discover *final* knowledge through *your own experience*.

The *Love* of the eternal cosmic Sun that gave you birth to be a radiant star, out of its own eternal essence, is now alive within you—in *your own* immortal form—and only through that *Love* will you attain the faculty that grants you final *in-sight*.

✺

Yet now, before descending once again to the domains of the external spheres of the material cosmos, and then, far lower still, down to the outer realm of *earth*, let us abide a little while inside this world of final causes, of ceaselessly creative generation, and behold its awesome wonders.

✺

With amazement you now recognize that here, where you before had seen no more than boundless seas of fire, flaring in all colors, you are in fact surrounded by a new reality, a world of elemental, primal forms.

Now you see that all things here consist of form-imbuing energies, which must themselves be given form, so that they can in turn continue to create new figurations.

For now, all this to you still seems mere *chaos*, and so you do not know how to make sense of what you see.

But soon you will be able to unravel this complexity; the more you learn to *use* your *inner eye*.

Much that here surrounds you like mysterious hieroglyphs you then will see revealing its enigmas. And in this realm you also shall, at last, detect the "key" that will unlock the chains you had to bear on earth, as an incarnate human self in physical existence.

Thus shall your inmost essence be "unlocked" and opened to your spirit!

✺

Inseparably connected by a web of myriad interweaving threads, innumerable images of life unfolding in the inmost realm of causes here continue to display their workings to your eyes.

You still perceive all this as merely "images," in that your faculty of apprehending the domain of final causes is not yet developed. Also, habit forces you to translate all things you encounter into *images* before your *understanding* can absorb them.

In truth, however, what you witness here is simply the activity of those eternal forces of creation, anchored in the Origin, whose workings constitute the final cause of *all reality* that ever came into existence.

That is why you here can also rediscover, and learn to comprehend, all things that ever came to be. Indeed, until you learned to know what *can* be apprehended in this realm, all your earthly "knowledge" has woven for you merely dark, deceptive veils, on which your rife imagination paints the answers that must hide your ultimate unknowing —from yourself.

*

The inner sense you now possess—a sense in which all other faculties are *unified as one*—shall soon be able to distinguish individual forms among the manifold complexities of what you witness as a whole.

Realities unfolding at the origin of all creation shall here reveal themselves in their successive phases before your inner eye.

Events removed from you by whole eternities you shall observe as taking place *at present*.

All concepts and ideas that ever human minds were able to envision are merely *shadows* and *reflections* of what you here behold *existing in reality*.

You must have clearly grasped this truth before this world of colorful abundance will admit you to its inner secrets.

Do not look back to life on earth, attempting by comparisons to find the key to understanding what in itself remains *unique* and can be comprehended only through its *own* inherent forms.

You will be seeing colors, signs, and forms that may at times resemble things on earth; even so you ought not to compare if you would not confuse with other things a realm of which there is *no second*, which is without *equivalent*.

You here must learn to understand the elements of a new language; and only when its sounds awaken corresponding echoes in your soul will you begin to fathom what it has to tell you.

Books of ancient sacred knowledge you possess on earth bear witness of that language, but your distance from the wisdom of their authors was too great, and so you came to put your own interpretation on the insights of the ancient sages.

When here now you have learned to comprehend that language, you shall later be amazed and smile at your naive complacency. You then will find it hard to grasp that earlier the wording of these books had seemed to you like dark enigmas, and that you felt you had the right to offer "explanations" where wiser minds than you had meant to give you *final clarity*.

In very truth, "The word of God goes forth through all the earth"; but one must first have learned to *apprehend* the *sound* of that eternal word before one would interpret the *meaning* of its language.

Had not so many in their deafness speculated on the meaning of these texts, there would no doubt be less confusion in the world today.

*

There is no force, no energy throughout the infinite expanse of cosmic "space" that could not manifest itself to your perception both as *sound* and *sign*.

Where we are now, however, all senses of perception are unified within *one single integrated sense*; and so you here experience also sounds and signs within *one unified perception*.

When here you can distinguish *form* and *color*, you will at once become aware that also feeling, taste, as well as scent and sound are consciously alive in you.

But since you are yourself a form created by the very elements you here observe in action, it follows that whatever you perceive in this domain must needs possess in you a corresponding echo.

Do not attempt to "read" some meaning "into" what you here observe, but seek instead to find a constant state of perfect inner calm and concentration—until the answer to your question comes to you *from your own self*.

Once you have received an answer, accept it without hesitation. Bear in mind, however, that everyone will here receive an answer that is exclusively his *own*, and that you would be sacrificing your insight's highest value if you sought to wait for others in order to compare the answers they received with yours.

Just as you were *by yourself*, and not with any other, when the primordial Sun, out of its eternal fires, gave you birth to be a radiant star, so can you also here attain to highest insight only *by yourself alone*. And yet, the knowledge you acquire in your own distinctive form is going to reflect the insights likewise of all others who in this realm had learned to know by virtue of the same perceptive faculty.

✼

Now do you understand why here I must not offer you interpretations of the forms and colors you perceive?

I thus would give you only *my interpretation*—from without—and thereby keep you from discovering the answer that is *solely yours*.

Yet nothing but the answer you have found *yourself* is able to awaken the very energies within you that you need if you would reach your ultimate perfection—in your *own distinctive form*.

Although we shall for now remain together, do not expect my explanations to shed light on things that *you* yourself must learn to answer—for things you must yourself have learned to feel.

✼ ✼
✼

REVIEWS OF CREATION

INFINITE ARE THE DIMENSIONS of the cosmic "sphere" wherein we seem to float, although that endless orb creates its own most distant outer "limits" by means of the innumerable hosts of suns and planets pouring from its center into timeless space.

Infinite are likewise the realities encompassed in this realm, and you would feel that all eternities are but a single day if ever you intended to explore the endless wonders of this all-encompassing existence.

You may have heard that "seers" lived on the earth in ancient times who, all too trusting in their finite mental powers, haughtily presumed to calculate the ages that a universe requires to attain its final form and, ultimately, to disintegrate again into the "uncreated void."

They clearly did not recognize their folly, nor seemed to know that wiser minds had lived before their day, whose witness they no longer understood. And so they acted rather like the child who, it is said, attempted to scoop out the ocean—with a little bucket.

※

Everlasting in the *final* sense—*without beginning, without end*—is the eternal "cosmic day" whose length those thinkers sought to measure. And likewise *everlasting*, at the same eternal time, endures the endless "cosmic night."

In its eternal EMANATION, the cosmic sun in whose primordial fires you were born to be a flaming star, continually sets the outmost limits of its active powers where all those galaxies of stellar worlds abound, which here surround us on all sides like faintly glowing nebulae encompassing a boundless sphere.

New stellar systems are eternally assuming form within the circle closed by all the galaxies already in existence. At the same time, other cosmic systems, containing hosts of suns and planets without number are constantly absorbed again into the measureless expanse of "space."

No calculations made by mortal minds can ever fathom, nor tangibly express, the aeons during which a single one of these galactic systems comes into existence, or once again disintegrating will return to nothing.

Revelation from the Spirit's world has never so demeaned itself that it would vouchsafe to reveal to mortal minds what must forever pass their comprehension.

Every insight granted human mortals from the realm of the eternal Spirit was, at all times, wisely measured in proportion to their faculties of understanding, and thus could be of practical effect and value, even in the darkness that surrounds their earthly lives.

*

You think it strange that *innermost reality* in the domain of final causes is being opened to your comprehension, while things in the *external realm* are to remain beyond your grasp?

But let your inner self direct you, and do not overlook that here you are in your eternal, erstwhile home, which you, eternities ago, had willfully abandoned, impatient to explore an alien sphere, although you knew full well that in the outer realms you would be able to assert yourself by virtue only of *effects*, not in your timeless being's proper essence.

It was your very greatness that once had caused your fall.

Even now you may *repeat* that *fall*, and thus delay your permanent return into the world of light again for aeons. And such a *second* fall into the realm of darkness has sometimes even been the fate of souls who once had pledged themselves to bear the same demanding burden that now weighs also on my shoulders—as a freely chosen task—in cases when they proved unequal to their very greatness.

For this reason was I sent to be your guide, lest temptation should mislead you.

Here, within the *innermost* domain of Being shall your own eternal "realm" take form, so that you may from this dimension once again effect events in your external world.

Here, you one day shall be active by virtue of the same creative force that is the *cause* of all external forms of life. In your external world, however, you now would only face *deflected* forces, whose power there exceeds your strength; for in your outer life you cannot manifest the energy inherent in your spirit's light.

Everything throughout the measureless expanse of "space" is consciously in full possession of its own potential and creative powers *solely* in its own exclusive sphere; it thus could not in any other place reveal the fullness of its powers.

Even the eternal Light of the Beginning is all-powerful within itself alone; yet all the infinite dimensions of creation continue pouring from its depth.

The farther from the core of the all-generating primal Sun, the more unlike its essence also grow the energies that it is sending forth; until, in the most distant outer sphere, the energies of *Being* transform themselves into the energy of *Counter-Being*.

Only here, in the *interior* of this boundless sphere, are we in truth within the realm of "God's" eternal essence.

When we descend again to the external stellar systems, in order to return once more to earth, we there shall find ourselves *removed* from life in this divine eternal essence—as measured from the vantage of material life—and only in our *inmost self* can we retain its conscious presence.

The Spirit's godlike power certainly pervades the most external realms as well, but in those outer realms the Spirit's might is not within its own domain, wherein it can reveal the fullness of its powers. Only those who have *awakened* in that inmost realm can, therefore, still detect those powers *in themselves*.

Still, if you have found that even earth's external nature shows you wonders you attribute to the "hand of God," you need to bear in mind that also the most distant outer realm originated, ultimately, from the innermost domain and, therefore, still retains the final traces of its source, the Light of the Beginning, despite the ever active force of *Counter-Being*.

In the external realm, however, your hands are going to be tied; for in that sphere the elements of *Counter-Being* are in their dominion and, consequently, the superior might.

You will at all times have to reach this timeless world of light by drawing on your being's innermost potential whenever in your outer life you would subdue those forces of resistance, even in some lesser matters; but you can never master them completely.

Fakirs, as well as power-hungry adepts of the occult arts endeavored to accomplish this in other ways. Through wearisome and endless exercises they subjugated certain forms of these elusive counter-forces and made them servants of their will. Yet never was there any found on earth who did not in the end, for all the occult powers that he mastered, fall victim to a wretched fate.

The *divinely sanctioned magi* of all ages have always worked from only this interior realm, and through the energies informed of God, which only here surround us. Tradition may have turned those sages into workers of external "miracles," but one never recognized the *real wonders* they performed, because these *wonders* are concealed to mortal eyes. The effects, by contrast, of their actions, which mortal eyes are clearly able to discern, shall not at any time reveal the real sources of their power.

It is *here* that you can find the signs that each one must have learned to use who is to be endowed with *magic* powers serving *God*. But none has ever found those signs who in his greed for hidden power craved the reputation of a "miracle worker."

Here, within this holy sanctuary, you have to learn to feel with *inner senses* what these dynamic signs would have you apprehend.

In this domain you truly need to feel at home again if your eternal origin is to entrust you with its treasures.

✶

IN PRINCIPIO ERAT VERBUM—In the Beginning was the Word—so it is written in a sacred book. And many a seeker since has racked his hapless mind to answer the unprofitable question why here the "Word" is raised to such exalted rank, and why the ancient sage identified the Origin of all Becoming as the "Word."

Yet it was profoundest *insight* that expressed such doctrine in that form.

The primordial Emanation of the Sun whose timeless fires radiate Eternal Love *voices* its own Self as never-ceasing impulse toward Becoming; it transforms its own Self into rhythmically articulated motion and becomes the cosmic Word of the Beginning, which summons all creation into being, after its inherent laws, which order magnitude and number.

Words that mortals speak in human tongues are but the faintest and most distant echo of the "Word that is with God," and which itself is *God* throughout the aeons without end.

The ancient sage refers to a "beginning" that forever *was* in progress and forever *shall* proceed.

Here you witness this "Beginning" rise before your inner eye, and so you see the "Word" reveal itself in forms and sound, in rhythm and in color, as the initial utterance of the eternal will that shapes all life throughout creation.

Abide a while and let your feelings search within your innermost, so that you may experience the profoundest essence of that Word of the Beginning, from which proceeded all things that have ever come to be, and which shall likewise be the source of all things yet to come.

✸

As LUX IN TENEBRIS—as light within the darkness—this eternal Word of the Beginning sends its voice into the measureless abyss of "space," and so brings forth, out of its proper essence, the first created primal forms. And, in shudders of awakening self-cognition, it feels impelled to build, already in this primal realm, an altar as a place of worship.

Configurations of primordial creative power surround this altar like a priestly chorus paying solemn homage. Crystallized as Being's first created forms, although still rigid in their bound condition, they yet embody images of silent prayer.

✶

Yet in this realm there is no standing still to contemplate what has already come into existence. And so you now behold how from this first primordial form the fullness of dynamic structures issues forth in boundless generation. You witness ever new configurations gaining shape; you see their outlines ebb and flow, continuously interweaving with each other until, amidst this endless wealth of forms in motion there arises, in increasing brilliance, the radiant gem in which the *Word* then knows itself, within the world its voice had summoned into being, and where it now reveals itself as manifested form.

And as the *Word* now triumphs as a brilliant light amidst the forms it has brought into being, there now rings forth, through all the Spirit's countless realms, the joyous chorus of the First Creation.

TE DEUM LAUDAMUS—to Thee, o Lord, we offer praise—this hymn intoned by form resounds through the eternal Spirit's first-created world, and all the spheres of heaven exult in solemn adoration.

Here has the *Word* become an *individuated Self* within its own creation, and all the Spirit's legions of created forms rejoice in jubilation, recognizing their own being's origin to have proceeded from that *Self*.

The radiant world of pure, all-generating *Spirit* has come into being, forever to revolve within itself, in all its boundless forms.

The Word of the Beginning thus effects expression of its innermost fulfillment!

✶

However, in this primal sphere of light, the *Word's* creative impulse, its will to call creations into being, has not yet reached the limits of its might.

For also this domain of innermost fulfillment has retained its power to bring forth, and will continue to engender forms within the measureless expanses of eternal "space." It thus will of itself establish and define the limits of its vast domain, and thereby bring about the cosmic *counterforce* to all eternal "space," to all eternal "time."

What in the Spirit's innermost domain is one and undivided, here it becomes duality, and so your spirit's eye beholds the likeness of a cosmic foundry of production in its evolution, wherein the unborn power of the Spirit forms and molds what are the underlying preconditions of the galactic stellar systems that here envelop us as distant nebulae embodying a giant sphere of light. Creative forces active in this realm bring into being SPACE AND TIME, such as it constitutes the universe of the external realm.

Here it has become unlike eternal "space," yet it continues to embody the latter's all-informing laws.

It is no more the Spirit's mode of "space," which *in itself* embraces all of time; instead, this newly shaped external space will bring forth time out of its own existence.

While here your timeless self essentially *pervades* eternal "space," even as you are yourself pervaded by its nature, *external* space, which generates external time, will everywhere confine you within limits.

Again, within eternal "space," your spirit's eye discerns as if it were itself a boundless sphere, which both contains all things that are, and sees each thing from every side at once; within *external* space you will be able to perceive in only one direction—from a point within yourself toward things that lie without—and always merely from a single, fixed perspective.

※

Only at this stage there now begins creation's *second* phase; the echo, as it were, of the Eternal Word, which, from its proper substance, had brought the *first* creation into being.

Darkness of the outermost dimension flows like waves that roil a boundless sea—yet then, "God's Spirit moves upon the waters," and the shimmer of its radiant light, imbued with infinite creative power, now immerses its dynamic will, the source of all becoming, into that cosmic sea of darkness. Here you behold an image of this PRIMAL GENERATION.

Magic signs descending from the Origin become transformed into configurations of external worlds. Darkness now will soon dissolve itself before your spirit's eye.

※

Within a dome-like vault of generating energies you see how SEEDS OF FUTURE WORLDS are gaining life and form.

Ceaselessly they pour into existence, while the sea of darkness brightens and transforms itself into a radiant cloud.

Already here you recognize how from these primal seeds EMERGING WORLDS are brought into existence. Form-endowing forces of primordial creation here pursue their ancient task, while cosmic luminescence drifts across created space like swaths of lucid haze.

Soon these worlds in evolution will have reached their final form.

✼

What you are now about to witness is the BIRTH OF THE ETERNAL COSMOS, the exiting of the engendered outer worlds from the dimension of the form-endowing forces of Creation.

Within the depth of everlasting night, infinities removed from the primordial Sun of Love that gave you birth to be a flaming star, global bodies have arisen in multitudes past counting —the outmost boundary the Word of the Beginning has itself established as the limit of its powers. These worlds now form the luminescent stellar haze that here encloses us on every side, high above us and below, expanding like a vaulting sphere of infinite dimensions.

✴

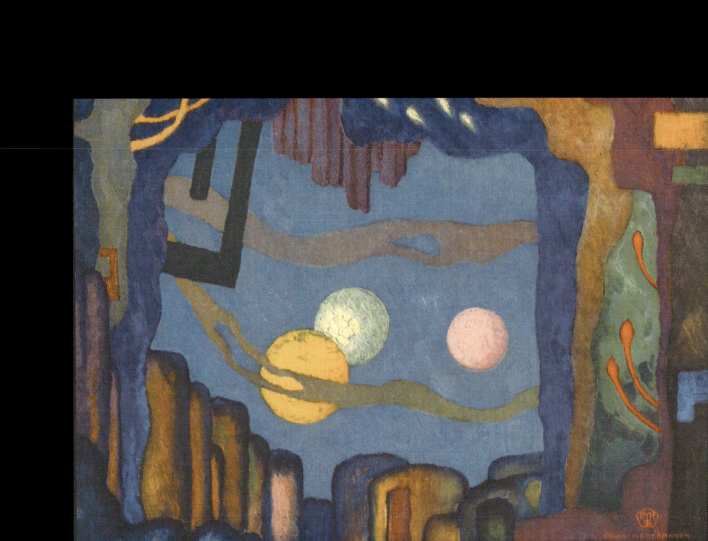

Now your inner eye will open to behold events that come to pass on one of those innumerable worlds, which henceforth live their independent lives.

Remember when I told you that, in all dimensions of created forms, nothing ever did, nor, for that matter, could occur, that one might not review within this realm of light, this sphere of primal emanations, in images reflecting final causes.

Here you now shall trace the toilsome paths the *fallen* human spirit must pursue on these external worlds, so that it one day can escape the folly of its will's direction and thus recover the capacity to will its own return into the light of its eternal home. For when the human spirit once had turned away from its primordial origin, determined to acquire self-experience in the external, outmost regions of that origin's Creation, that impulse caused the spirit's *fall*.

*

Initially, the human spirit merely finds on these external worlds a rigid, narrow LABYRINTH of brilliant colors, where every exit promises to lead it to an even brighter light, only to betray its hopes and expectations time and time again.

Exhausted, it at last will go no further; for it is forced to recognize that in its spiritual form it cannot here attain its freedom.

*

And so the human spirit feels consumed by the DESIRE FOR EXTERNAL FORM. As a result, a human self that once had known a state of all-surpassing *freedom* now seeks its place in the procession of the multitudes of beings who long for their external bodies on these outer worlds.

✸

Having finally attained material form in the external world—in the body of an animal—the spirit's eyes discover a new directive sign, which it believes will guide it rightly, but thus it only lets itself fall prey to the abhorrent sphere of ASTRAL LUMINESCENCE, whose ghastly light envelops each of those external worlds.

Although this luminescence is deceptive, its forces will possess the spirit that has entered their domain. Thus, as the captured spirit gropes its way from one delusion to another, it finally falls prey to guilt and, driven by despair to wanton folly, it scornfully denounces *light itself*—in any form.

*

Creature instincts now take full possession of the human being, and in orgies of unbridled frenzy—provoked by spiritual faculties in bestial perversion—the animal at last confronts the spirit with its SODOM.

*

Bereft of even its last fading hope, imprisoned on all sides by horrifying darkness, it gropes its way through an INFERNO, a hell of its own making, while terrors haunt the madness of its blasphemy, like furies.

Escape from this perdition appears no longer possible.

Shudders of relentless horror must the human spirit now endure, until despair at last awakens recollections of its former greatness, and it remembers that its timeless self is of *divine descent*.

*

Here, then, for the first time the spirit feels again that restless inner longing to make its way back to its origin. And this intent shall one day guide it back to its eternal home, which at this point still seems infinities beyond the spirit's vision.

Timidly and full of fear it tries to take the first few steps as it begins its journey home.

Nonetheless, the very glimpse that saving help is possible imbues the spirit's new desire with a hope that makes it tremble.

*

After agonies of all but endless searching, the human spirit finally discovers, in the midst of darkness, a source of light whose radiance it recognizes as belonging to its home.

With redoubled energy it now directs its still uncertain steps through the oppressive darkness toward that distant light.

After many efforts it at last succeeds in slowly getting closer.

In the midst of its inferno it now distinguishes a hidden sanctuary.

Already it believes salvation is at hand, but ghastly eyes repel it with demonic stare: the temple's threshold is protected by forbidding guards.

The spirit needs its last remaining strength, lest it succumb to deadly fear.

Countless times it ventures to approach the awesome steps, resolved to cross the temple's threshold.

Again and again it is repelled by horror of the guardians.

At last, however, its persistence is rewarded.

Out of the gloomy heights above, the spirit hears a voice, whose sound imbues its efforts with new strength.

Suddenly, it feels as if its hands were held by unseen guides; fearlessly it now can look into the monsters' threatening eyes and, like a conqueror in triumph, it proudly steps across the threshold.

✳

Now, within the sanctuary's inner halls, the spirit feels at once as if the *animal* component of its nature had fallen from it like a foreign garb.

Once again it feels it is a spiritual being and, rising from its soul's profoundest depth, words begin to form a prayer on its lips: DE PROFUNDIS —"From the abyss, O Lord, redeem my soul!"

The spirit bows in adoration before the image of the Godhead, which it now beholds within the temple's radiant depth.

Prayer here becomes its first experience of salvation from unbearable ordeals.

✵

But when at last it lifts its eyes, the spirit apprehends a new, more radiant brightness shining from behind the image of the Godhead, and it feels how unseen hands are drawing it to enter that refulgent hall.

With timid and uncertain steps it cautiously advances.

Here, too, there will be threats and perils to confront, but now the spirit feels no longer any sense of fear.

At last, the final curtains part and now, as peals of thunder echo through the air, the spirit's eyes behold in radiant splendor the precious gem of REVELATION.

Memories of ages long forgotten now are reawakened. And so the spirit feels as if it had returned again to that dimension in the Spirit's realm where it had once heard also its own voice among the jubilant celestial hosts proclaiming their "Te Deum."

*

Barely able to contain its joy, it now approaches that resplendent gem, which in turn transforms itself, before the spirit's eyes, into a *sun*, whose brilliant light disperses and defeats the last concealing veils.

Here, at last, the human spirit has attained the fullness of ILLUMINATION and its total essence is pervaded by the Spirit's light.

*

Its timeless being now perfected as a source of purest light, the human spirit thus surveys the path it has completed. Here, then, shall it witness how, from the depths of the primordial Origin, the cosmic energies that bring forth all Creation come to build the lofty sanctum of a temple. And as in its most sacred shrine, the slowly parting veils reveal the holiest of visions to the spirit's eyes, it apprehends, in even richer splendor, a jewel far more brilliant even than the precious gem that it had contemplated at the *Revelation* of the Godhead's image.

Here, at last, the human spirit finds the ultimate FULFILLMENT of its highest longing.

*

At this point, however, it desires to return to the external earth; for now it knows that, in its earthly form, it can achieve "salvation" only by its *physically expressing* the eternal Spirit's life that has awakened in its inmost self.

It now has grown aware that *physically embodying* the Spirit's substance is the "key" that will unlock its earthly bonds forever, so that it henceforth may pursue its mortal life as one whose self is *free*; as one who has been born a *child of Light*: a redeemer of its own eternal self and of its human fellow spirits; a helper, thus, of those who also had, unseen and unsuspected, helped it to ascend its own path to salvation.

*

Inspired by such lofty, pure resolve, the human spirit finds itself, at almost the same instant, high upon majestic peaks, where, from the depths of jagged cliffs and hidden valleys, light appears to burst like sheaths of flaming arrows.

Everything its eyes behold appears ablaze in golden light, and in each ray it feels the triumph of its VICTORY.

✳

But the victor cannot linger if he would secure the fruits of his success.

Towering above its vantage point the spirit now beholds a mountain range of even more majestic height, whose gleaming summits are forever covered by eternal snow.

The tabernacle guarding the Eternal on this planet has revealed its presence to the spirit's eyes.

It clearly feels: the distant peak of purest white that shines amidst a sky of flaming gold is HIMAVAT—the sacred mount where those alone have their abode whom the *primordial Light of the Beginning chose itself* to be its consecrated kings and priests on earth.

What here it sees is the *primordial image* of that rumored legendary temple and its guardian knighthood; here is the factual *reality* of which a faith-inspired myth had once brought word to Western lands, in forms that people at the time could comprehend, by telling them about the *holy grail*.

*

That temple site is now the goal toward which the spirit makes its way.

Although aware that on this path there still are obstacles and dangers to surmount, the spirit knows it is expected, and that its guide is waiting at that temple, to lead it through this earthly life. And, once its time has been fulfilled, that helper also shall unlock for it the portal, so that it may, like you, find back again the way to its eternal home.

The viscous masses of retarding, dull *inertia* that it first encounters are determined to impede its stride. One look, however, toward its goal is all it needs to master that obstruction.

Doubts, assured of easy victory, arise before the spirit like a palisade of jagged rocks, ready to benumb its courage. Yet at this point no might on earth could any longer hold it back; and even were it bleeding from a thousand wounds, it surely now will overcome this last remaining hindrance.

Having reached its goal, after a demanding, all but endless journey, it hardly will think back on the travails it suffered on the way.

One shall receive that spirit as a being that has *found its timeless self*, and crown it with the golden wreath of knowledge.

It shall be clothed in sacred linen of the purest white, lest any blemish that had stained it on the way should any longer mar its garment.

Thus it shall be consecrated to the will of the *Eternal*, and become initiated in the sacred *Royal Art*: the faculty of *physically embodying*, in mortal human likeness, the Spirit's living *substance* through the highest form of Love.

What until then had been benighted *creature life* shall be transformed within the spirit's nature, and all its earthly faculties will henceforth only serve to manifest the Spirit's light.

It shall be taught to understand that, in the Spirit's life, only courage can retain the crown of its eternal realm forever; that it is cowardice, or fear-deluded folly to flee the world of mortal senses: the very sphere to which the human self's own will had once desired to submit.

✶

Yet, saying this, I have already touched upon the things that I am now about to tell you, given that you have been born, within the Spirit, as a radiant star.

In truth, what until now your opened inner eyes have shown you was nothing other than *your own* eternal path, from when your timeless self abandoned its eternal home to its eventual return, which caused it to become the flaming star, such as you now appear before me.

One with me, your spiritually connected inner guide, you now will often find yourself within this inmost realm of Spirit, to witness ultimate reality, and see its marvels pass before your eyes. The visual perceptions that the Source of all Becoming will reveal to you, however, shall every time be new and different.

But always bear in mind that the "phenomena" you here observe at all times only show you *realities of living spiritual essence*; and that these "images" are in effect the *archetypal patterns* of all activity throughout Creation, whereof on earth, in that remotest border realm of cosmic Being, you never witness more than a deformed reflection.

※

We now return to earth, which is in need of your triumphant light.

Let not sadness cloud your inner radiance, nor grief find entry in your soul when we now leave this realm of living light and, having once again returned to earth, you sense the spiritual darkness which there encloses you on every side.

Whoever has returned to life on earth like *you*, no longer needs to fear the threat of night; for he now bears his own light *in himself*: the Light that is eternal.

Your sole concern should henceforth be to let the light you now possess illuminate all aspects of your earthly life; and, as a star—born in the primordial fire of the Spirit's Sun of Love—to be a *light* to all who still are lost in darkness.

Desire nothing any longer *for yourself*, and all things you have need of shall be given you: by virtue of *your own light's inner power*.

You cannot let one ray of your own light fall on the hearts of others that would not gain you hearts in turn a hundredfold.

It will not cost you any *effort* to let your light be *seen*. You only must take care that, through your actions in your earthly life, you never will *obscure* the true Light of Eternity, which would illuminate your being, and thus to darken its reflection in the sight of others.

If you will but entrust *your own self* wholly to the light now born within you, its rays will so pervade the body also of your earthly life that it shall cast no shadow any longer on the paths of those who need your light to guide them in the darkness of their mortal lives.

✳

My company, however, you shall find whenever you have need, even should our mortal bodies live on different continents, separated by vast oceans.

You must not seek me in my earthly, mortal garb; for in the realm of physical existence I never could unite myself with you the way we now are one: within our beings' innermost.

You must *yourself* descend into your feelings' *inmost depth* if you again would apprehend my presence; and every time you shall once more behold this realm of light—of *radiant spiritual substance*—you likewise can perceive it only within the *innermost dimension* of your being.

✳   ✳

✳

EPILOGUE

I SEE YOU AS A READER moved by love to search for light and inner clarity, which you expect this book to give you. Thus, I would not have you be misled to think that anyone has ever found such clarity and inner light by merely *reading* and reflective *thought*.

The insights that I here transmit disclose the *Way*, the *Truth*, and the *Life*, but if you would receive them, they must become the way, the truth, and the life *within your very being*.

To let you see what you shall come to know if you are willing to pursue this goal, I here have purposely gone far ahead of where you stand at present, in the attempt to waken in you, in anticipation, feelings and perceptions you shall experience in tangible reality only after you have entered, and courageously resolved to scale, the path I have attempted to illuminate in all my writings, from every point of view, in such a way that no one can mistake it. I here can only sketch an outline of the path one must already have completed, in its given stages, before one can attain the spiritual maturity which, in the present book, already is assumed at the beginning of the "Guidance."

Nonetheless, I have good reasons to assert that, on the path ascending to the Spirit, any kind of fetter may prove harmful, even the securing tether of a guide.

Every human spirit here on earth is born with its unique capacities of self-expression, and each will thus most safely undertake its quest in its own special way—even in the footsteps of its guide.

And so you should not form the false impression that you must be familiar with my other writings before the present book could motivate you to begin the search for the eternal path within yourself that leads to timeless freedom.

There are temperaments who will not set out on a journey unless they first have carefully examined, on a map, the smallest detail of the expedition, evaluating every turn, each elevation and decline along the road—and there again are others, who merely need to visualize a goal, and then decide spontaneously to enter on that journey, without concern for the conditions of the route.

Similarly, then, the former may employ the books in question as a kind of "map," while the others may consult them only later, as companions on their quest.

But since the nature of the task I have been given to accomplish in this day demands that everything I can provide, with the expressive means at my disposal, should constitute an integrated unity, one must not separate even the present book from anything I have already said, or may still publish in the future.

The pathway to the Spirit has been so deeply buried under rockslides of ungrounded thought that even the most earnest and courageous seekers may despair of ever finding it. Indeed, many are today of the opinion that all things ever mentioned in the course of human history pertaining to this quest were simply hopes of pitiful illusion.

Just as, at the foot of Alpine peaks, the traveling stranger finds himself surrounded by a host of guides, each promising to take him to the summit, even so are those who seek the way into the Spirit in our time besieged by voices on all sides, and every caller swears by all things holy to lead the seeker to his goal.

All too many put their faith in guides who have themselves no knowledge of the way, but never have I met a person who in this fashion reached his goal.

Little wonder that the path into the Spirit then is said impossible to find, and that the few who truly found it, having followed knowing guides, often meet with sympathetic condescension, as if they were the victims of deluded piety.

Thus, the need is great to show the present age that, all this notwithstanding, a path into the Spirit truly does exist, and that all those who will pursue that path are certain to attain their goal.

To be sure, the reader who would undertake this quest will need a measure of intuitive *discernment*; for one should not pursue this path, which, after all, is not devoid of danger, unless one feels the guidance offered evokes the same degree of conscious trust which naturally awakes in every human spirit when it faces competent direction; unless, of course, a person will no longer listen to what that inner voice may have to say.

Many also hesitate to take this path because the gloom of baneful doctrines has, through the millennia, weighed upon all mankind like a nightmare, creating the impression that the path into the Spirit is a life of world renunciation, self-denial, and voluntary suffering.

Such doctrines have inflicted untold evils on mankind; their venomous delusions led to sacrilege against the holiest domain of life; and even now their fury rages unabated.

Mankind truly paid too high a price for the sublime and venerable causes in the name of which such a disastrous harvest has been nurtured.

One doubtless acted in good faith when thinking that the path into the Spirit could not be attempted but at the price of "giving up the world." And to this day one clings to that belief.

Yet no matter how emphatically one stressed the putative necessity of "renouncing" the world in order to attain the Spirit, it was not long before the advocates of all such doctrines found themselves compelled, albeit with much moaning and lament, to yield substantial ground to the demands of life—the very wellspring flowing from the Spirit—which truly is more powerful than any creed or dogma.

Moreover, one ought not to assume that such ascetic doctrines truly represent the pure and uncorrupted wisdom of mankind's greatest teachers.

The sole exception one might mention in this context is that famous Indian prince who saw no other way of rescuing his decadent society than by his sermons on the grief and suffering that weigh upon man's mortal life, from which one could gain liberation only by renouncing worldly aims.

Yet even in this one exceptional case there are compelling grounds to question whether such ascetic doctrines did not gain the form in which they are transmitted only after they had fallen prey to schools of monks, who thus promoted their own fame as "holy men."

Wherever in some other doctrines the infectious plague of quietistic indolence and fantasies of world rejection have been nurtured, one may be certain that such notions only represent misunderstandings of enlightened wisdom.

Already in the second century of our era voices did speak up, lamenting that the records which preserved the life and teachings of the great Master of Nazareth could no longer be regarded as *authentic*.

And how much more did minds of well-intentioned simple faith not add to and remove from these accounts in later ages!

Even so, however, some authentic traces have survived to our day; yet what they show is anything but an ascetic teacher praising world renunciation! And here it would be futile to appeal to "holy writ," seeing that this very scripture lets the Master frown on being called a "glutton and wine bibber," because he ate and drank with those who had invited him. The same scripture, in fact, that shows him changing *water* into *wine*—as the first of his recorded "miracles"—at a marriage, when, according to the "ruler of the feast," the guests had been already drinking quite enough.

If anyone has eyes to read, yet cannot see how the deluded advocates of world renunciation here must struggle with the Master's real teachings—a battle evident on every page of the transmitted records, but one that had been fought before the texts emerged we know today—for him there may not be much help.

Spread by a malignant source, a diabolical confusion of human thought and feeling has, through ages out of mind, affected succeeding generations across vast regions of the earth, ensnaring mortal minds in the perverse delusion that access to the Spirit's world is something one can, as it were, secure by purchase or by barter. As if there loomed a hidden potentate, exacting tribute from a firmly rooted earthly life, and keeping all from entering this path who proved unwilling to renounce this physical existence.

But as long as there continue to be human spirits who, by choice of their own will, have forfeited their "paradise"—and now must live embodied in a mortal creature form on earth, before they can retrace their way into the Spirit—their task shall always be to follow the divine command, "Subdue the earth and have dominion of its riches!" For only as their lives' unquestioned masters are they able, by virtue of enlightened efforts, to fortify the inner energies they need in order to pursue the way into the Spirit, under the protection of their guides.

Those who flee from earthly life, instead of learning how to master its potential, in truth have anything but "overcome the world."

You would ridiculously *overrate* the pleasures granted us by virtue of our living in a creature body, if you regard them as so precious that they might serve as fitting "payment" for your spiritual enlightenment.

You thus transform your God into a simple-minded savage who can be cheated of his gold by trading it for beads of glass.

To be sure, to *dominate the earth* does also mean to master its enjoyments. But *mastery* has never meant *renunciation*.

Like someone whose entire being is so occupied by a consuming task that, even in a noisy crowd, he only hears the voice within his soul, also you should thus not try to drown the clamor of your creature drives by shouting even louder, but through all their restless tumult you must learn to only hear *yourself*.

Hidden energies lie deeply rooted in your earthborn drives. You often enough grow conscious of their presence, when you surrender to their power, perhaps more frequently than you would wish.

But these forces want you as their master; and if you are unable to subdue them, but strangle them instead, you merely kill your most effective servants.

Being master of your earthborn drives implies that you are able to entrust yourself to what they crave—at any time, and of your own free will—without concern that they might carry you beyond the limits you set down.

Once you have accomplished that, you will have gained the highest measure of resilience your mortal life can grant you for your spirit's further growth.

You cannot find your way back to the life of your eternal *spiritual* essence unless you make effective use of all the energies that are at your disposal in this *present* form of being, given that you now are born into a creature body.

Whatever else you may be told is merely idle dreaming, without foundation in reality.

Many have in this way fashioned "inner worlds" composed of dreams. Although these often may display the beauty of a poet's inspiration, they rest upon no other truth than that expected in poetic fiction.

Others thought *ecstatic rapture* allowed them to approach their timeless self and they in fact became convinced of having found it in this way.

They did not realize that in this way they had succumbed to a delusion, induced by hidden energies inherent in their mortal bodies: energies they had awakened and unleashed, but had not learned to master.

If I may here advise you, as one who speaks of things he knows in all their depth, my counsel would be this: Stay clear of every path that rests on mystical delusions, or validates its "knowledge" by "clairvoyant" proof. But more than any other, avoid all teachings tempting you to take the path of ecstasy, which leads you to surrender your *conscious self-control and will.*

The Spirit of Eternity, from which your inmost self descends, and in whose light it once again would find its timeless home, is the most *absolute reality* among all things one might define as "real."

Never shall that Spirit manifest itself to minds that dream or worship phantoms.

You need to seek that Spirit in yourself with no less clarity of mind, with no less fervent dedication than that demanded even of researchers striving to discover forces whose existence they suspect within *external nature.*

But do not search in places far away!

Your task is, after all, to find the *inmost* life within you.

Most who claim their search had been in vain had drifted far afield, convinced they had to find some wholly new and different experience. But in this way they had themselves obscured from their own eyes the very inmost essence of their being, which was, and ever will be, closer to them than all else.

Only *in yourself*, within the inmost of your *inner self* begins the path that leads you back to your eternal origin and home.

To be sure, if you would find that inner path you will have to devote a little time each day to quiet contemplation. Bear in mind, however, that this will benefit you only if it will enrich and strengthen the activities your daily life demands of you, not if it paralyzes your existence.

Whoever, in his quest of innermost reality, does not experience how, at the same time, all his energies to meet his earthly tasks and duties are slowly growing day by day, that seeker follows paths that lead him in the wrong direction.

The path into the Spirit's living light is in reality so *simple, so uncomplicated,* that you are well advised to *simplify*—to radically *un-complicate*—your inner life, your thinking and your feelings.

That is the meaning of the words the venerable Master spoke when he declared, "Unless you receive the kingdom of God *like a child* it shall not be revealed to you."

The mental life of most today has grown to be so complicated that they have lost the faculty to apprehend the mystery of human nature, and therefore need to make a conscious, earnest effort to react to intuitions of the simplest kind.

Although the ways are many that you may employ to reawaken yourself to a spiritually conscious life, once having reached your goal, you will be quite amazed that you had failed to recognize much sooner what you shall then regard as the most obvious, self-evident, and simplest thing on earth.

You are not separated from the Spirit's living essence *even now*; it is only that the simple, integrated *power of perception*, which could reveal that life within you, still lies dormant in your consciousness. And since you are mistakenly convinced that one can enter *spiritual reality* by means of intellect and thought, you make no effort to awaken that unique perceptive faculty within you, which would shed light on all your questions, if it already were awake.

What you are given in this present book are means whereby you may awaken this perceptive faculty.

Your inner consciousness needs to be *tuned*, even as one tunes a *harp*, so that the pure, all-unifying *primal chord* may resonate within you; for it alone can wrest that power from its sleep.

Even if at first it dare reveal its presence in you only timidly and faintly, once your consciousness has truly heard its voice, you cannot ever lose it any more.

Yet do not think that this awakening could somehow be induced by force!

What you can do is simply to create, each day anew, the needed preconditions for this to occur, and then you patiently must wait until, sooner or later, it shall reveal itself within you of its *own volition*.

The most important factor in this preparation is seeking to maintain, in all expressions of your will and mind, a state of sensitivity that is responsive to the *uttermost simplicity*.

"Blessed are the poor in spirit; for theirs is the kingdom of heaven."

Your mind is still encumbered by a staggering wealth of mental ballast, which merely hampers the required ease and freedom of your stride. You must preserve your full mobility, however, if you expect to find the "kingdom of heaven" that is in you.

Only in this sense should you "abandon" and "renounce" yourself and all you own, in order to be able to regain your real self, awake in the dimension of reality. For you have long since made your thoughts a substitute of your true nature, unaware that your enduring self is something very different from your capacity of thinking, which all but suffocates you in its wealth.

But you must prove yourself the *master* also of your *thoughts*; even though today they rather treat you as their helpless slave.

I here need to remind you of what I told you earlier, when speaking of the drives inherent in your earthly creature:

Being *master* does not mean relinquishing the *service* of one's *subjects!*

But never must your *servants* make themselves your *master*.

Imbue your heart with steadfast, quiet confidence; for if you would achieve a goal you must above all else believe in your own self, and in your power to attain it.

Do not begin your quest by asking endless questions that must remain unanswered until you shall have learned to *live* your life according to the insights that I give you.

What this quest demands of you are *deeds* and *active mastery* of your *external life*. And the result such conduct brings about will be a different *state of being*, not just another change of your ideas and ways of thinking.

For now, do not concern yourself with anything you may have thought, accepted, or believed until this day.

If you transform what I am giving you into productive *deeds* and *life*, you one day shall be able to determine for yourself what in your present thinking rests on truth, and what misled you as illusion.

If you cannot find the answer to a question in *yourself*, that question is not truly answered, in the final sense, even if you hear another person's answer.

Within *yourself* alone must all your being, life, and thought experience its profoundest ground and proof.

Consistently maintain an inner state of *calm serenity* in every situation of your outer life; and if you cannot yet accomplish this today, then seek to train yourself to that effect.

You will object that your external life confronts you every day with incidents not even a philosopher could bear with patience and serene detachment.

I readily agree with you that, from your present point of view, your judgment seems undoubtedly correct.

However, you will learn to see these matters in a different light when you are able to *transform* the *orientation* of your *inner being*.

The events and matters of this earthly life are never more, nor less, to us than what we choose to make of them in our minds.

I certainly would not expect that having to endure a tragic fate, or grievous suffering, should leave your inner calm and balance unaffected.

The weighty things in life, however, seldom will disturb your inner calm. Indeed, it may be said that not a few have come to know the inner stillness I advise you to maintain, precisely owing to their having suffered pain and grief.

More often it will be the little, trivial things of daily life that typically disturb your peace of mind; matters and events that very soon again become quite unimportant.

Given that you are not meant to flee from your external life, you need to cultivate a state of mind and soul that lets you face the problems of your daily life with patience and composure.

In the external realm of this existence there is not much that you can change, even if the changes you would make might prove a boon to all mankind.

Only in *yourself* are you endowed with nearly unrestricted power; and you will feel this power growing in you with increasing force, the more you learn to use it in your inner life.

No potentate has ever been so foolish that he thought he could demand the same degree of loyalty in foreign lands to which he was entitled only in his proper realm.

You likewise ought not to expect from life *without* what you are able to control and order, according to your wish and will, within *your inner world alone*.

To be sure, external things may always, at first impact, upset your inner balance for a moment. Even so, the second moment should already find you in control again, forcefully imposing calm on all the elements within you that had not readily submitted to your first command.

With such practice will you spare yourself much sorrow and vexation, and thus become your own source of enduring joy.

In order that you may transform yourself into your own experience of profoundest joy, to that effect I offer you whatever help and guidance you may need.

My aim is to awaken the creative *artist* in your nature, who has the power to transform your being into an eternal image of the Godhead.

In this transformation, you are yourself at once the *artist* and the artist's *work*.

It has been far too long since the creative artist in your nature sought to lend your essence lasting form; and so you have forgotten that no one but yourself can ever fashion the eternal form you shall possess.

You always judged the form that random chance had forced upon you from without to be the work of inescapable necessity.

Of this delusion I would like to see you free.

Whatever good or ill the stars may have allotted to your earthly life, all that is not some iron "fate" whose chains you cannot break. Instead, it should inspire you at all times to exert yourself wisely to subordinate both positive and negative endowments to the service of your highest good.

The *artist* in your nature works with the material he is given, even as he finds it. His mastery reveals itself, however, in his skill of integrating both the strengths and imperfections of the means at hand to the unique advantage of his work.

Yet to accomplish this, you must begin to feel the *artist* of that work *within you*, even if until this day you were convinced that meeting the demands of life required less an artist than the dry approach of an accountant.

What you may gain by heeding my advice are treasures without limits. At the same time, you can rest assured that in so doing there is truly nothing you could lose.

Teach yourself to use this book the way it should be used and it will benefit you greatly in your quest.

Yet not from merely glancing at its pages may you hope to reap such benefits, but only when your *reading* will transform its contents into personal *experience*.

Then, however, I believe this book will grow to be a trusted *friend*; a friend whose company you will no longer want to miss, and who will consecrate your earthly home, transforming it into a *temple*.

The more you learn to let your *inner senses* feel the spiritual perspectives I have shown you in this book, mindful of the precepts of my guidance, the more distinctly will you also sense the final meaning of my *words*. Even as the *words* would guide you to make the images your own, by letting them express their language in your soul.

May words and images alike enrich your life with blessings! *May you, then, by your own efforts gain the virtue to be equal to the exhortation that the priesthood of an ancient sanctuary had inscribed above its entrance:*

KNOW THYSELF!

REMINDER

"Yet here I must point out again that if one would derive the fullest benefit from studying the books I wrote to show the way into the Spirit, one has to read them in the original; even if this should require learning German.

"Translations can at best provide assistance in helping readers gradually perceive, even through the spirit of a different language, what I convey with the resources of my mother tongue."

From "Answers to Everyone" (1933), *Gleanings*. Bern: Kobersche Verlagsbuchhandlung, 1990

For a complete listing of the author's works, including the titles that have appeared in English translation, and a brochure on his writings, his name, and biography, readers are invited to contact The Kober Press or visit its Internet site:

The Kober Press
2534 Chilton Way
Berkeley, California 94704, U.S.A.

Phone: 510-540-7309
Fax: 510-548-2411
Email: koberpress@mindspring.com
Internet: http://www.kober.com

LIST OF ILLUSTRATIONS

Emanation, 62 × 92 cm, page 27

In Principio Erat Verbum, 62 × 92 cm, page 32

Lux in Tenebris, 60.5 × 85 cm, page 35

Te Deum Laudamus, 62 × 92 cm, page 36

Space and Time, 39 × 50 cm, page 38

Primal Generation, 60.5 × 91 cm, page 41

Seeds of Future Worlds, 35 × 50 cm, page 43

Emerging Worlds, 35 × 49 cm, page 44

Birth of the External Cosmos, 50 × 70 cm, page 47

Labyrinth, 50 × 60 cm, page 48

Desire for External Form, 35 × 55 cm, page 51

Astral Luminescence, 75 × 46.5 cm, page 52

Sodom, 50 × 60 cm, page 55

Inferno, 62 × 52 cm, page 56

De Profundis, 52 × 67 cm, page 61

Revelation, 52 × 68 cm, page 62

Illumination, 59.5 × 45 cm, page 65

Fulfillment, 62 × 93 cm, page 66

Victory, 60 × 91 cm, page 69

Himavat, 60.5 × 90 cm, page 70